LIFE WITHOUT ANIMALS

# WHAT IF PRAIRIE DOGS DISAPPEARED?

By Theresa Emminizer

**Please visit our website, www.garethstevens.com. For a free color catalog of all our high-quality books, call toll free 1-800-542-2595 or fax 1-877-542-2596.**

**Library of Congress Cataloging-in-Publication Data**

Names: Emminizer, Theresa, author.
Title: What if prairie dogs disappeared? / Theresa Emminizer.
Description: New York : Gareth Stevens, [2020] | Series: Life without animals | Includes index.
Identifiers: LCCN 2018060877| ISBN 9781538238189 (paperback) | ISBN 9781538238202 (library bound) | ISBN 9781538238196 (6 pack)
Subjects: LCSH: Prairie dogs–Conservation–Juvenile literature.
Classification: LCC QL737.R68 E46 2020 | DDC 599.36/7–dc23
LC record available at https://lccn.loc.gov/2018060877

Published in 2020 by
**Gareth Stevens Publishing**
111 East 14th Street, Suite 349
New York, NY 10003

Copyright © 2020 Gareth Stevens Publishing

Designer: Laura Bowen
Editor: Theresa Emminizer

Photo credits: cover, p. 1 Joe Grabo/Shutterstock.com; pp. 3-24 (series art) De-V/Shutterstock.com; p. 5 Frank Fichtmueller/Shutterstock.com; p. 7 ESK Imagery/Shutterstock.com; p. 9 ZoltanTarlacz/Shutterstock.com; p. 11 iliuta goean/Shutterstock.com; p. 13 dean bertoncelj/Shutterstock.com; p. 15 (owl) Voodison328/Shutterstock.com; p. 15 (jackrabbit) Danita Delmont/Shutterstock.com; p. 15 (rattlesnake) Mark_Kostich/Shutterstock.com; p. 17 Peter Gudella/Shutterstock.com; p. 19 Jaren Jai Wicklund/Shutterstock.com; p. 21 Marco Specht/Shutterstock.com.

All rights reserved. No part of this book may be reproduced in any form without permission in writing from the publisher, except by a reviewer.

Printed in the United States of America

CPSIA compliance information: Batch #CS19GS: For further information contact Gareth Stevens, New York, New York at 1-800-542-2595.

# CONTENTS



**Boldface** words appear in the glossary.

## Small But Mighty

Prairie dogs are **rodents** that live in central and western North America. They can stand 15 inches (38 cm) tall and weigh about 4 pounds (1.8 kg). But don't let their size fool you! These little animals are important. What would happen if they disappeared?

## Grassland Habitats

There are five species, or kinds, of prairie dogs: black-tailed, Gunnison's, Mexican, Utah, and white-tailed. They live in **habitats** called grasslands, or open areas of land covered in grass. They eat grass, plants, roots, and seeds. They live in large groups called colonies.

## Prairie Dog Towns

Prairie dogs build **burrows** called dog towns. Towns are made up of long tunnels and rooms where prairie dogs sleep, raise their young, keep food, and go to the bathroom. The biggest-known prairie dog town was 25,000 square miles (64,750 sq km)!

## What Harms Prairie Dogs?

Prairie dog habitats are shrinking. During the 1900s, their Great Plains habitat was taken over by farms. The prairie dog **range** shrank to just 5 percent of what it had been. Within that time, most of the black-tailed prairie dogs were killed by people.

Farmers see prairie dogs as pests because their burrows can harm crops. Farm animals can step in burrows and get hurt. Prairie dogs are often hunted and their burrows are plowed up. They are also harmed by illnesses, such as the **bubonic plague**.

## Why Are They Important?

Prairie dogs are a keystone species. That means many other species in their **ecosystem** need them to **survive**. Prairie dogs help about 150 other species. Their dog towns become homes for jackrabbits, owls, rattlesnakes, salamanders, swift foxes, and toads.

burrowing owl
jackrabbit
rattlesnake

By digging up the earth and eating many plants, prairie dogs keep the soil healthy for new growth. This growth draws bugs to the habitat, which birds eat. Prairie dogs are also a key food for many predators, including coyotes, hawks, and ferrets.

## What Will Happen?

The number of prairie dogs is dropping. If they disappear, their ecosystem will be out of balance. Species that use prairie dog burrows would lose their homes. The numbers of **endangered** black-footed ferrets and other predators that hunt prairie dogs could fall.

## Saving Prairie Dogs

Once there were hundreds of millions of prairie dogs across North America. Overhunting and people taking over their habitats must be stopped before it's too late. Helping people understand the importance of prairie dogs will be a key part of making sure this keystone species survives!

# GLOSSARY

**bubonic plague:** a dangerous disease, or illness

**burrow:** a hole made by an animal in which it lives or hides

**ecosystem:** all the living things in an area

**endangered:** in danger of dying out

**habitat:** the place or type of place where a plant or animal naturally lives and grows

**range:** the area where something lives

**rodent:** a small, furry animal with large front teeth, such as a mouse or rat

**survive:** to live through something

# FOR MORE INFORMATION

## BOOKS

Bodden, Valerie. *Prairie Dogs.* Mankato, MN: Creative Education, 2019.

Gish, Melissa. *Prairie Dogs.* Mankato, MN: Creative Education, 2018.

## WEBSITES

**National Geographic Kids**
*kids.nationalgeographic.com/animals/prairie-dog/*
Learn more fun facts about prairie dogs.

**Wild Earth Guardians**
*wildearthguardians.org/wildlife-conservation/protect-prairie-dog-empires/*
Find out how you can help prairie dogs.

**Publisher's note to educators and parents:** Our editors have carefully reviewed these websites to ensure that they are suitable for students. Many websites change frequently, however, and we cannot guarantee that a site's future contents will continue to meet our high standards of quality and educational value. Be advised that students should be closely supervised whenever they access the internet.

# INDEX